Common Core

El

By

Published by Gallopade International, Inc.

Printed in the U.S.A. (Peachtree City, Georgia)

TABLE OF CONTENTS

G: Includes Graphic Organizer

GO: Graphic Organizer is also available 8½" x 11" online download at www.gallopade.com/client/go

(numbers above correspond to the graphic organizer numbers online)

What Is Electricity?

Read the text and answer the questions.

What comes to mind when you think about electricity? You might describe electricity as "shocking" or even "powerful." You could also describe electricity by what it does. Electricity greatly affects how we live, work, and play. Electricity lights up our homes, powers our computers, and keeps us warm or cool. Electricity from batteries powers our cars, our flashlights, and our cell phones too.

[1]Electricity is very useful, but it can also be very dangerous. [2]Do not go outside during a thunderstorm. [3]Lightning is a very powerful form of electricity that can strike and hurt people. [4]In your school or home, be careful when plugging or unplugging electrical devices. [5]Touching an electrical outlet can shock you and cause serious damage to organs like your heart, lungs, and brain.

In science, electricity is defined as a form of energy caused by the movement of electrons. Electricity comes in two different forms. Static electricity is caused by friction and is the build-up of electrons in one place. Static electricity can be released as a zap of electric current, like lightning. Current electricity is electricity that flows in a current like water in a river. Current electricity usually flows through something from one place to another.

1. Match the following questions to whether they are best answered by paragraph 1, 2, or 3 of the text.
   A. _____ What is electricity?
   B. _____ Why is electricity sometimes described as "shocking"?
   C. _____ Why is electricity important?

2. Read each sentence in the 2nd paragraph and identify whether the sentence is a declarative sentence (**D**) or an imperative sentence (**I**).
   1st _____ 2nd _____ 3rd _____ 4th _____ 5th _____

3. Use the text to define electricity.

4. A. What are the two forms of electricity?
   B. Explain how each form of energy works.
   C. Which form of energy is better for lighting a light bulb? Explain why.

Using Electricity

Read the journal entry and answer the questions.

Today I woke up to my alarm blaring loud music. I was so tired, but I had to get up! I stumbled into the bathroom and turned on the light. Then I ran the shower water until it got hot. After my shower, I dried my hair with an electric blow dryer. That didn't take long, since I just got a haircut!

I headed downstairs to the kitchen, turned on the light, and grabbed some milk from the refrigerator. I popped some toast into the toaster and reheated a slice of ham in the microwave oven. As I ate, I turned on the television to check the weather. Then, I suddenly remembered to print out the history report I did last night on the computer. I raced upstairs to brush my teeth with my electric toothbrush, and ran out the door to meet my friends at the bus stop!

1. Write an appropriate title to express the main idea of this journal entry.
2. Complete the graphic organizer by identifying at least 8 ways that the author used electricity.

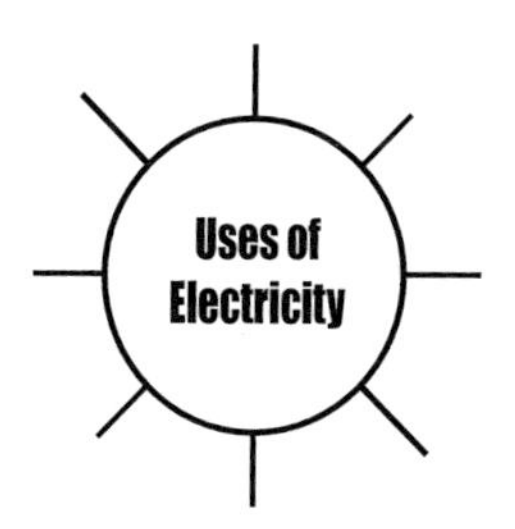

3. Complete the graphic organizer by classifying each use of electricity as producing either heat, light, sound, or motion. *(Some uses may be listed in more than one category).*

Heat	Light	Sound	Motion

Electrons

Read the text and answer the questions.

All matter is made up of tiny particles called atoms. Atoms are made of even smaller particles called protons, electrons, and neutrons. Protons carry a positive charge (+), electrons carry a negative charge (–), and neutrons carry no charge. Neutrons and protons are held close together in the atom's nucleus (center), but electrons have freedom to move in orbit around the atom's nucleus. Sometimes, electrons can even jump from one atom to another.

Most atoms have the same number of electrons and protons, which makes them neutral, or balanced, with no charge. Atoms are naturally neutral, but atoms can gain and lose electrons. An atom with more protons than electrons is positively charged. An atom with more electrons than protons is negatively charged.

When atoms have a positive or negative charge, they try to gain or lose electrons to get back to neutral. As electrons move from one atom to another, they transmit energy from one place to another. This movement of electrons, and energy, is called electricity. By using generators, batteries, magnets, and conductors, we can start and control the flow of electrons between atoms into a current of electricity that is useful to people.

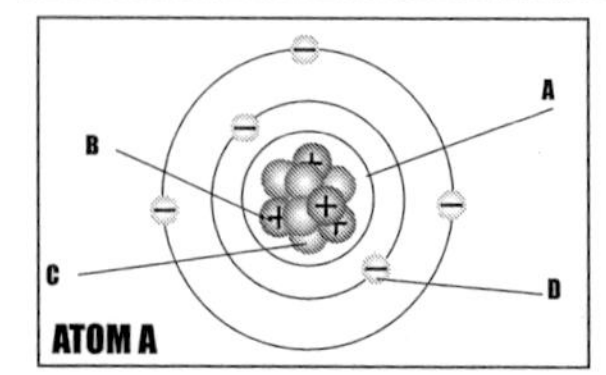

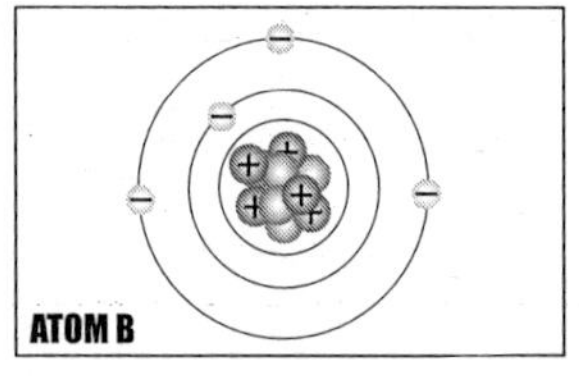

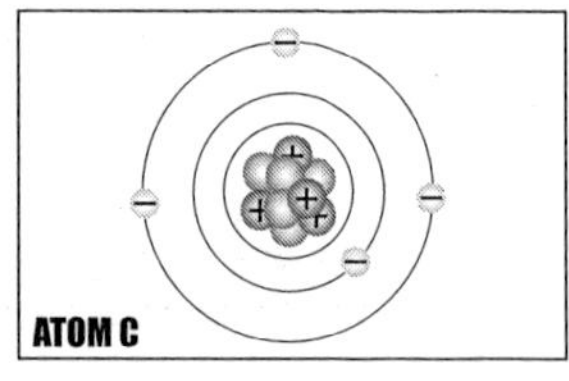

1. A. Identify each part of "Atom A" (A, B, C, and D) in the diagram.
   B. Is the charge of "Atom A" positive, negative, or neutral? Explain.
   C. Is the charge of "Atom B" positive, negative, or neutral? Explain.
   D. Is the charge of "Atom C" positive, negative, or neutral? Explain.
2. Define balanced as it is used in the text.
3. A. What will a positively charged atom attempt to do? Explain.
   B. What will a negatively charged atom attempt to do? Explain.
4. Describe the relationship between electrons and electricity.
5. Is electricity best described as the creation, flow, or use of energy?

Static Electricity

Read the text and answer the questions.

Static electricity is an <u>imbalance</u> of electrons in an object or on an object's surface. It occurs when two objects touch and electrons jump from one object to the other. The object that gains electrons becomes negatively charged (–). The object that loses electrons becomes positively charged (+). Friction and dry air make static electricity more likely to occur.

When objects have opposite charges, they attract each other. When objects have the same charges, they repel (push away) each other. This affects what happens when static electricity is created.

If you rub a balloon on your sweater, the balloon collects some of the electrons from the sweater. The balloon gets a negative charge and the sweater gets a positive charge. If you touch the balloon back to the sweater, the balloon sticks to it because the balloon's charge is opposite of the sweater's charge. The balloon also takes electrons back from the sweater to get back to "<u>neutral</u>."

If you slide your sock-covered feet as you walk across a carpet, your socks will collect electrons from the carpet. The extra electrons cling to your body until they can be released. When you touch a doorknob or another person, the electrons <u>discharge</u>, jumping off your body as a tiny bolt of electricity. Ouch!

1. Give a synonym for each word as it is used in the text:
   A. <u>imbalance</u> B. <u>neutral</u> C. <u>discharge</u>
2. "Static" means "no movement." Make inferences from the text to explain why this type of electricity is called "static" electricity.
3. How do friction and dry air affect the movement of electrons?
4. For each **effect**, list a direct **cause**:
   A. Electrons jump from one neutral object to another neutral object.
   B. An object becomes negatively charged.
   C. An object becomes positively charged.
   D. An object with a positive or negative charge becomes neutral.
5. In the example in the text, will the balloon continue to stick to the sweater after the balloon becomes neutral? Explain why or why not.

Lightning Bolt!

Read the conversation between Mark and his science teacher. Then complete Parts A and B.

[Thunder RUMBLES]

Teacher: I can almost feel the static in the air!

Mark: What do you mean by that?

Teacher: Lightning is really just a big static electricity spark.

Mark: But lightning is so powerful...how can that be?

Teacher: Remember how you learned that when two things rub together, like when your feet drag along carpet, some electrons move from one object to the other, creating static electricity?

Mark: Yes, and when you touch another object, like a doorknob, the extra electrons in your body flow out, and ZAP!

Teacher: That's right! Well, lightning works a lot like that.

Mark: How does that happen in the sky?

Teacher: Good question! Winds inside a rain cloud blow in all directions. Water droplets are pushed up high in the cloud, where they freeze, then frozen droplets are pushed down in the cloud, crossing paths with raindrops moving up. As the raindrops and ice pass each other, the ice takes some of the electrons from the rain drops. This causes the top of the cloud to become positively charged and the bottom of the cloud to become negatively charged, creating static electricity. When the static electricity gets strong enough, the extra electrons find a place to go, and lightning occurs!

Mark: I get it! It's like when you touch a doorknob! Hmmm, but where do the extra electrons go?

Teacher: Sometimes the lightning occurs high in the sky, as electrons go from one part of the cloud to another, or from one cloud to another. Sometimes, the negative charge in the cloud is so strong it pushes away electrons in the ground, making the ground positively charged. The cloud and the ground are like your hand and the doorknob. The electrons race from the cloud to the ground to neutralize the charge in the cloud with the charge on the ground. This process heats the air, a spark ignites, and ZAP—*lightning*.

PART A: Use the text to answer the questions.

1. Complete each analogy: *(ex. Hot is to sun, as cold is to ice.)*
   A. Cloud is to ground, as hand is to ___________.
   B. Feet are to carpet, as frozen ice are to ___________.
2. For each **cause**, identify the **effect**:
   A. Wind in a raincloud blows in all directions.
   B. Air heats up when electrons move from a cloud to the ground.
   C. The negative charge in a cloud causes the ground to become positively charged.

PART B: Read the poem and answer the questions.

The Countdown

Boom! Crack! Four...
I run quickly to my door!
Pitter patter, pitter patter—rain
Tapping at my window pane.

Boom! Clap! Three...
I open the door to see!
Wind kicking up dust
The swing set creaking with rust!

Boom! Crackle! Two...
So powerful are you!
Wind, fierce and frightening!
Rain never stopping!

Flash! Bang! Fire! One!
I surrender! You have won!
I run and hide from your dreadful song
Lightning dances all night long!

3. What event is being described in the poem? How do you know?
4. What does the "The Countdown" in the poem represent?
5. Analyze writing style and literary devices in the poem:
   A. Identify at least five examples of onomatopoeia.
   B. Identify one example of personification.
   C. Is the poem written in present tense or past tense?
   D. Is the poem written in first-person or second-person?
   E. Describe the mood of the poem.
6. Describe how the author of the poem changes from the beginning of the poem to the end. Why do you think that change occurred? Cite evidence from the text to support both answers.
7. A. Which text is more effective at helping you "see" and "feel" what is happening in a lightning storm? Why?
   B. Which text is more effective at helping you "understand" what is happening in a lightning storm? Why?

The Kite Experiment

Read the texts and answer the questions

"The History and Present State of Electricity," written by Joseph Priestley in 1767, was based on Priestley's research and interviews with many scientists, including Benjamin Franklin. This text is a paraphrased selection from Priestley's manuscript.

"The Doctor first thought to test his hypothesis on the sameness of lightning and electricity by building a spire on [Christ Church] in Philadelphia. Through the rod he could direct lightning down from the clouds.

"But, it occurred to him that a common kite might have better access to the regions of thunder and lightning. Preparing a kite with a key attached to the string, he took the opportunity of an approaching thunderstorm to take a walk in the fields. Because he was worried of the ridicule that often comes from an unsuccessful attempt in science, he told only his son of his plans, who assisted him in raising the kite.

"When the kite was raised to the clouds, the Doctor observed that loose threads of the string stood straight up, as if avoiding one another. Struck by this promising sign, he immediately presented his knuckle to the key, and the discovery was complete. Benjamin Franklin felt a very evident electric spark.

"When the string became wet from rain, the key collected incredible amounts of electric fire."

1. Use the text to identify who or what is being described:
   A. "The Doctor"
   B. "promising sign"
   C. "regions of thunder and lightning"
   D. "electric fire"
2. A. What did Benjamin Franklin believe about lightning?
   B. Describe the two methods Franklin devised to prove his theory.
3. Describe the purpose of each of the following: (in Franklin's experiment)
   A. the lightning rod
   B. the kite
   C. touching his knuckle to the key
   D. the experiment with the kite
4. A. What were the results of Franklin's experiment?
   B. Was his hypothesis proven correct? Explain.

Conductors and Insulators

Read the text and answer the questions.

CLASSIFIED ADS

Job Title: Conductor
Job Description: If you allow electrons to flow freely in a strong current, this may be the right job for you. No prior experience necessary, but you must be able to conduct electricity through your body from one place to another. If you are a metal, salt water, or graphite, you have a very good chance of getting this job. Humans are capable conductors but should not apply for this job, because electricity often has harmful, even deadly, effects on the human body.

Job Title: Insulator
Job Description: You must be the opposite of a conductor. Your atoms must be stable and able to block the flow of electricity. If you get this job, you could find yourself in a variety of products. You will also be used in homes and businesses to protect people from the harmful effects of electricity. If you are plastic, Styrofoam, paper, rubber, or glass, you have a good chance of being hired.

1. Is the meaning of the text literal or figurative? Explain why.
2. A. What is the purpose of a conductor?
   B. What is the purpose of an insulator?
3. Describe how electrons differ between a conductor and an insulator.
4. Determine whether each example is a conductor or an insulator:
   A. A rubber tube wrapped around an electric wire
   B. A copper wire that connects a battery to a light bulb
   C. A metal rod that directs lightning from the sky to the earth and away from people and their homes
   D. A glass bulb that surrounds an electric light
   E. Rubber gloves worn by an electrician
5. Is the human body better categorized as a conductor or an insulator? Explain why.
6. Choose an electrical appliance such as a lamp or a computer. Make a diagram of it and label parts as either conductors or insulators.

Batteries

Read the text and answer the questions.

Did you know that electricity can be produced through chemical reactions? It happens every day—with batteries! A battery is a kind of tiny power plant that converts a chemical reaction into electrical energy. Batteries allow us to get electricity without having to "plug in." That way we can use our electrical devices wherever we are.

A battery is made of two or more metal plates, typically copper and zinc, called electrodes. In between the two electrodes is a salty solution called an electrolyte. When a battery is connected to an electrical device, a chemical reaction occurs between the two electrodes. Electrons pass between the electrodes through the electrolyte. This constant exchange of electrons creates an electric current that can be used to power electronic devices like flashlights, cell phones, and tablets.

Most batteries are primary cells. Primary cells eventually use all of their chemical energy and run out. Some batteries, called secondary cells, are rechargeable. When connected to an electrical outlet, electrical energy from the outlet recharges the battery's chemical energy so the battery can be used again and again.

1. What form of energy is used to create electricity from a battery?

2. Complete the chart by writing the purpose of each part of the battery.

Part	Describe It!	What Does It Do?
Electrode		
Electrolyte		

Determine whether each word best describes a primary cell (**PC**) or a secondary cell (**SC**) battery.

A. _____ rechargeable C. _____ disposable
B. _____ dead D. _____ reusable

3. Analyze the text, and use logical thinking and creativity to answer:
   A. What factors determine how long a battery lasts?
   B. How could a battery be made to last longer? What is the problem with this solution? Can you think of any other ideas? Problems?

Electrical Innovators

Read the text and answer the questions.

In the 1700s and 1800s, scientists began to understand more about the nature of electricity. Understanding led to inventions and improvements throughout these many years, as scientists often built on the ideas and discoveries of other scientists.

Then, in 1831 English scientist Michael Faraday discovered "electromagnetic induction"—the scientific name for moving a magnet inside a wire coil to produce electricity. This discovery led to the invention of the electric motor. Improved versions of Faraday's invention are used in millions of electric devices today—including air conditioners, refrigerators, electric stoves, computers, televisions, and much more.

American scientist Thomas Edison invented over 1,000 inventions during his lifetime. In 1879, Edison used his scientific knowledge of electrical conductors and currents to build the first practical light bulb. Running electricity through thin material, called a filament, makes it glow, and Edison tested many materials, including more than 6,000 plants from around the world, to find a material that was bright and that did not burn out too quickly. By the time Edison died in 1931, entire cities were lit by electric bulbs!

1. Summarize the text by describing the 5 W's of each inventor:

   A. Who was the inventor?

   B. What did he invent?

   C. When did he invent it?

   D. Where was he from?

   E. Why is this invention important?

2. Describe the effects of each inventor on the world today.

Faraday	**EFFECT:**
Edison	**EFFECT:**

3. *"Genius is one percent inspiration and ninety-nine percent perspiration."* Explain the meaning of Thomas Edison's quote as it relates to his life. How is this quote relevant today?

Electricity

Complete the graphic organizer by describing sources, identifying characteristics, and explaining the effects of electricity.

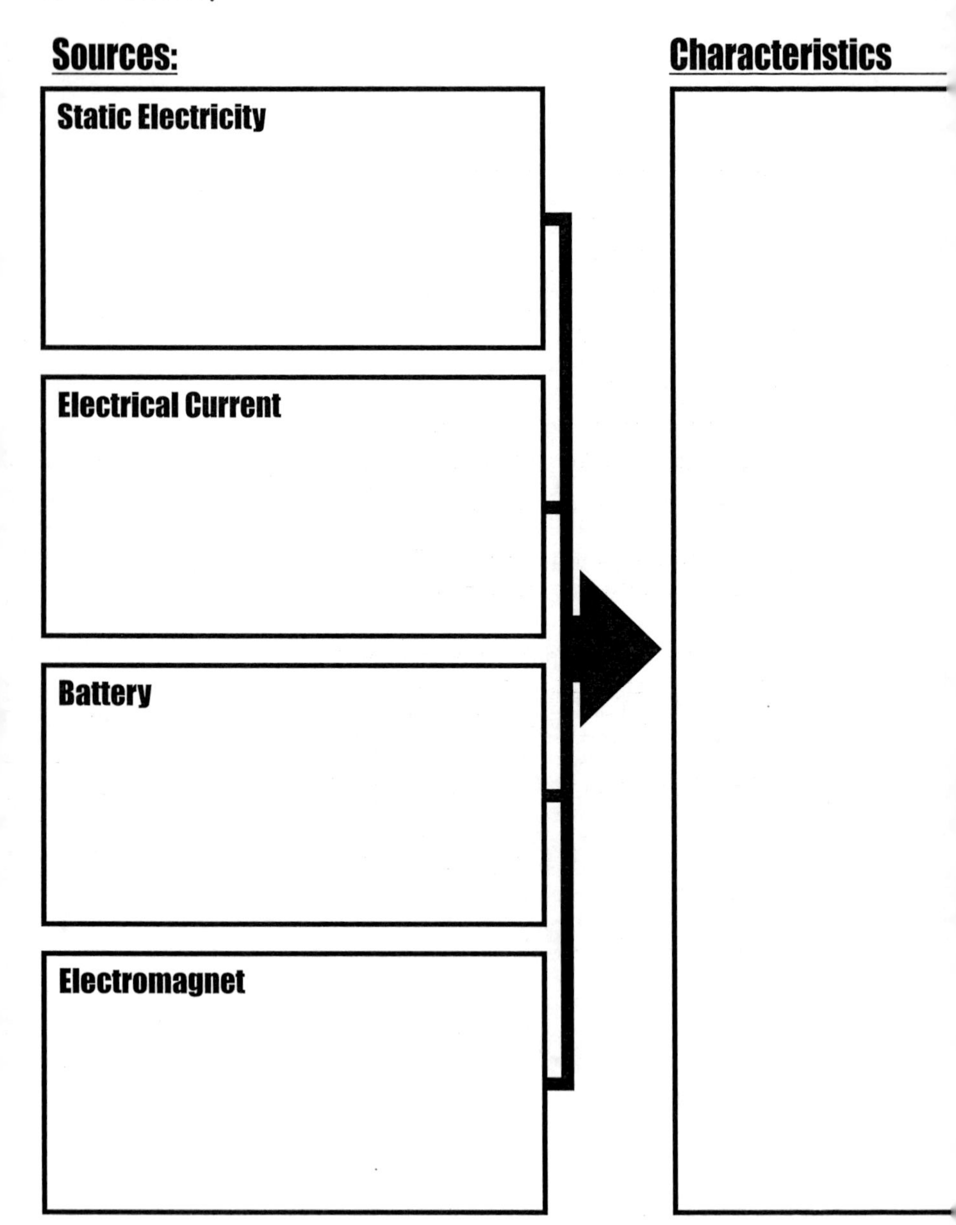

of Electricity

Effects:

Measuring Electricity

Read the text and answer the questions.

Electricity is measured in volts, amps, and watts. The potential strength of an electrical circuit is measured in volts. Many small toys use 1.5-volt AA batteries, because toys just need a little power to operate. A car, on the other hand, probably has a 12-volt battery. Electrical outlets in your home are likely 120-volts.

The flow of electricity in a current is measured in amperes, or amps. Amps are the measure of how many electrons are passing through a current at a certain point.

Watts are a measurement of the amount of work done by an electrical current. The wattage of an electrical current is related to its voltage and amps (Watts = volts x amps).

To imagine how these measurements work together, picture how water flows through a garden hose. Force (*voltage*) is applied when you turn on the faucet—the further you turn on the faucet, the more you increase the force. Next, the amount of water flowing through the hose is like the amount of electricity flowing through an electric current, which is measured in *amps*. And finally, the amount of work you can do with the water from the hose is like the *watts*—you can get more water on your plants if the water is flowing more quickly and with greater force. Similarly, a light bulb that has more watts will shine brighter than a light bulb with fewer watts.

1. Complete each sentence with volts, amps, or watts:
   A. Increasing the flow of electrons in a wire increases the _______.
   B. A car battery has more _______ than a AA battery.
   C. The higher the volts and amps, the higher the _______.
2. Which light bulb does more work—60-watt bulb or a 100-watt bulb?
3. Match volts, amps, and watts to the appropriate analogy.
   A. __________ The amount of work you can do with the water
   B. __________ The amount of water flowing through a hose
   C. __________ The force of water from a faucet through a hose
4. Draw a diagram that shows the flow of electricity from a battery to a light up toy and label volts, amps, and watts.

Electrical Inventions

Read each quotation and answer the questions.

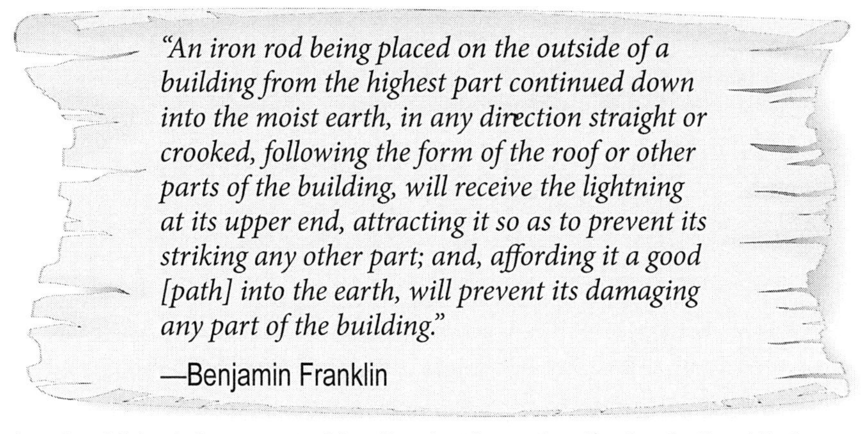

"An iron rod being placed on the outside of a building from the highest part continued down into the moist earth, in any direction straight or crooked, following the form of the roof or other parts of the building, will receive the lightning at its upper end, attracting it so as to prevent its striking any other part; and, affording it a good [path] into the earth, will prevent its damaging any part of the building."

—Benjamin Franklin

1. A. Make inferences to identify what invention Benjamin Franklin is describing.
   B. What is this invention designed to do?
   C. Draw a picture to show how this invention might work.

2. Place a ✓ next to the word that best describes the purpose of this invention. Support your answer with evidence from the text.
   a) _____ communication b) _____ safety c) _____ comfort

"Watson, ... if I can get a mechanism which will make a current of electricity vary in its intensity, [like] the air varies...when a sound is passing through it, I can telegraph any sound, even the sound of speech."

— Alexander Graham Bell

3. A. Make inferences to identify what invention Alexander Graham Bell is describing.
   B. What is this invention designed to do?
   C. How does this invention use electricity?

4. Place a ✓ next to the word that best describes the purpose of this invention. Support your answer with evidence from the text.
   a) _____ communication b) _____safety c) _____comfort

Circuits

Read the texts and answer the questions.

An electric current needs two P's to flow: a *push* and a *path*. The *push* is a source of electricity that makes electrons move. For example, a push can come from the chemical reactions in a battery, or from a generator, whose magnet causes electrons to flow.

The *path* electricity follows is called a circuit. The path is made of conductors that allow a current of electricity to flow. The path, or circuit, allows electricity to flow from a power source to devices that use electricity, such as light bulbs, fans, and motors.

A circuit's path can be <u>open</u> or <u>closed</u>. In order for electricity to flow, a circuit must be closed, meaning that all parts of the circuit are connected and unbroken. Electricity cannot flow through an open circuit because in an open circuit the path is incomplete. When you turn on a light switch in your home, you are closing a circuit and allowing electricity to flow. When the light switch is off, the path is open, and electricity cannot not flow.

PART A: Use the first text to answer these questions.

1. Match each of the following statements to whether they are best answered by paragraph 1, 2, or 3 of the text. Then use the text to answer each question.
   A. What causes electricity to flow?
   B. How can electricity be turned on and off?
   C. What allows electricity to move?

2. A. Label the *push* in the diagram.
   B. Label the *path* in the diagram.

3. Explain how you could interrupt the flow of electricity from the battery to the light, shown in the diagram.

4. For each situation, determine if the circuit is <u>open</u> (**O**) or <u>closed</u> (**C**):
   A. _____ You press the power button and the TV turns on.
   B. _____ You turn the light on but nothing happens—a bulb is broken!
   C. _____ Before fixing the electric wires in your home, the electrician turns the electricity off at the "electrical breaker."

There are two different types of circuits: a series circuit and a parallel circuit. In a series circuit, the electrical devices in the circuit are lined up one after another in a series. In a parallel circuit, each device is on a separate branch of the circuit.

Imagine a circuit with the following components: a battery, circuit wires, and two light bulbs. In a series circuit, both bulbs share the same circuit of electricity. Because both bulbs are drawing power from the same circuit of electricity, each bulb receives less voltage, making both bulbs dimmer. Unfortunately, if one light bulb breaks, the circuit of electricity is broken, and neither light bulb can work.

In a parallel circuit, each light bulb is connected to the battery by its own separate branch of electricity. If one light bulb is broken or burned out, the others can stay lit. However, a parallel circuit uses more electricity than a series circuit and causes the battery to run out of energy more quickly.

PART B: Use the second text to answer these questions.

5. Identify each diagram as either a series circuit or a parallel circuit.

A ____________________

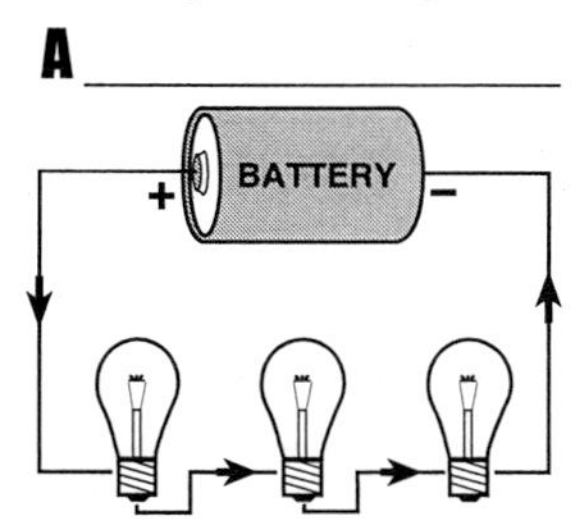

B ____________________

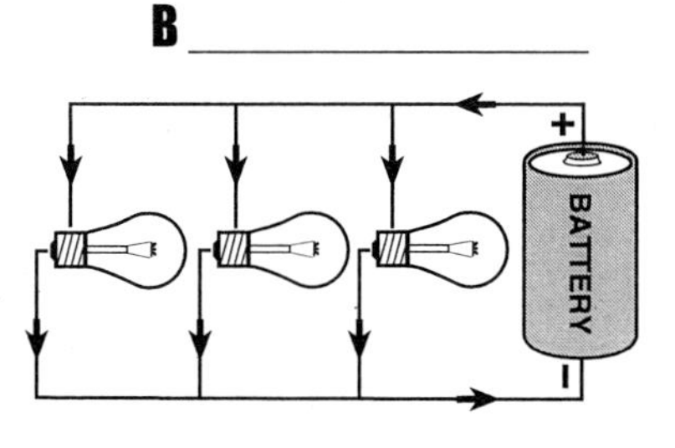

6. Complete the table by identifying the pros and cons of each circuit.

Type	Pros	Cons
Series		
Parallel		

PART C: Imagine you are putting up a string of festive lights at your house. When you plug the lights in, none of the lights turn on!

7. A. What could be the problem?
   B. What kind of circuit was most likely used in the lights?

8. Describe a type of circuit that could avoid this problem.

Building Circuits

Read the texts, look at the chart, and complete Parts A, B, and C.

Electrical devices, such as lights and fans, get their power by being connected to a circuit. Some electrical devices, such as light bulbs, have a fairly simple circuit, but some devices, such as computers, have complex circuits inside them to direct power to various places inside the device where it is needed. Before building circuits, engineers draw circuit diagrams to show what the circuit will look like. Circuit diagrams are used for building houses, schools, cars, and electronic devices like computers.

A circuit diagram shows the path electricity will follow. A circuit diagram also shows what other components the circuit will have. Circuits usually include an electrical device, such as a motor to produce motion, a microphone or buzzer to produce sound, or a light bulb to produce light. Additionally, a circuit usually contains a switch that closes (turns on) or opens (turns off) the circuit, so that the flow of electricity can be stopped or started.

Common symbols used in a circuit diagrams to represent the components of a circuit:

Light Bulb	Battery	Motor	Microphone
 —⊗—	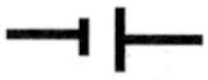 ⊣ ⊢	 —(M)—	
Buzzer	**Circuit Wire**	**Switch (closed)**	**Switch (open)**
 ○	 ——	●——	●—/

PART A: Use the text and chart above to answer these questions.

1. What is a circuit diagram?
2. What types of information are usually included on a circuit diagram?
3. A. What is the purpose of a switch?
   B. What would occur if a circuit did not have a switch?
4. List two ways the information in the chart would be used.

PART B: Look at the two circuit diagrams and answer the questions.

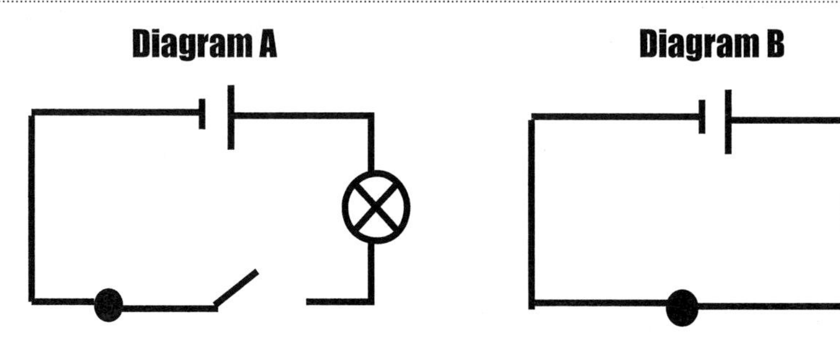

5. A. Label the components represented in each diagram.
   B. Which component is the source of electricity?

6. A. In which diagram would the light be on—A or B? Why?
   B. In which diagram would the light be off—A or B? Why?

7. These circuits could be found in what type of electronic device?

PART C: In addition to the first text and the chart, read and use the instructions for building a circuit to answer the questions below.

INSTRUCTIONS FOR BUILDING A CIRCUIT

1. Gather all the components that you will need.
2. Connect first circuit wire from the positive side of the battery to the fan.
3. Connect second circuit wire from the fan to the light.
4. Connect third circuit wire from the light to the switch.
5. Connect fourth circuit wire from the switch to the negative side of the battery.
6. Turn on the switch to test the circuit.

8. List the items that would be gathered in Step 1.

9. Draw a circuit diagram based on the instructions above.

10. When would a circuit diagram usually be drawn? Why?

11. A. What is the power source in this circuit?
    B. What device(s) will this circuit operate?

12. A. Is this a series circuit or a parallel circuit?
    B. What effects does that have?

Generating Electricity

Read the texts and answer the questions.

Method 1:	Method 2:
1) Water falls from a high place with great gravitational force. 2) The falling water hits and turns a turbine. 3) The turbine's motion rotates a magnet around wire in an electrical generator. 4) The generator produces an electric current.	1) Coal is burned to create heat that causes water to boil and turn into steam. 2) The steam rises and turns a turbine. 3) The turbine's motion rotates a magnet around wire in an electrical generator. 4) The generator produces an electric current.
Method 3:	**Method 4:**
1) A solar panel collects the sun's light to create heat that causes water to boil and turn into steam. 2) The steam rises and turns a turbine. 3) The turbine's motion rotates a magnet around wire in an electrical generator. 4) The generator produces an electric current.	1) Atoms of plutonium are split in a nuclear fission reactor, releasing heat energy that causes water to boil and turn into steam. 2) The steam rises and turns a turbine. 3) The turbine's motion rotates a magnet around wire in an electrical generator. 4) The generator produces an electric current.

1. For each Method in the text, determine the original source of energy. Create a table that summarizes this information.
2. A. Which Methods use heat as part of the process.
   B. Describe the role of heat in generating electricity.
3. A. How is the use of water in each method similar?
   B. How is the use of water in each method different?
4. What is the purpose of the turbine in each Method?

Make inferences to determine which Method best fits each description below. Explain your reasoning for each choice.

A. generates electricity fastest
B. generates electricity slowest
C. causes most pollution
D. causes least pollution

PART B: Read the text, look at the graph, and answer the questions.

1) Dear State Senator,

2) I recently discovered alarming information about our state's electricity production. As you can see, our state has many sources of electricity. However, most of the electricity in our state is made by burning coal.

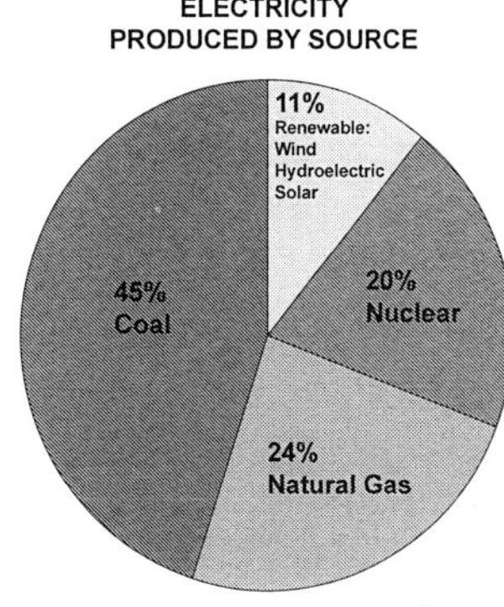

3) I think you will agree that the use of coal is a great hazard to the environment. Burning coal for electricity releases sulfur dioxide gas into the air. Too much sulfur dioxide in the atmosphere can be poisonous for humans, plants, and animals. Sulfur dioxide from coal mixes in clouds to produce acid rain that can damage plant, animal, and human habitats. Additionally, coal is a non-renewable resource that, once used up, will be gone forever.

4) There are many other sources of renewable energy, including wind, solar, and water that could be used instead of coal. These resources will not be used up and run out. And they don't cause much, if any, pollution.

5) In conclusion, I strongly urge you to use your role in our state Congress to support businesses that provide clean, renewable sources of electricity.

6) Sincerely,
Julie Johnson, a concerned citizen

1. A. What is the stated purpose of the letter?
   B. Why does the sender want to achieve that purpose?
   C. Describe the relationship between the sender and recipient.

2. A. What specific problem is the sender concerned about? Why?
   B. How does the sender support her opinion about the problem?
   C. How does the sender think the problem should be solved?
   D. How does the sender support her opinion about the solution?
   E. In your opinion, is the sender's argument effective? Why or why not?

3. Describe the organization of the letter by explaining the purpose of each section of the letter, 1-6.

4. Why does the author include the circle graph? Explain your choice.
   a) to be artistic b) to suggest a solution c) to give factual evidence

5. Create a circle graph that will replace the one in the letter if the sender is successful in generating the change she would like to see.

Electricity and Magnetism

Read the text and answer the questions.

Did you know that you really cannot separate magnetism and electricity? That is because an electric current creates a magnetic field. Similarly, a moving magnetic field creates an electric current. In fact, the electricity in your home and school is produced by a generator that uses spinning magnets to start the flow of electricity.

In the 1800s, scientists found that the needle on a compass moved when it was near an electric current. From this, they concluded that an electric current creates a magnetic field around the wire. Other scientists found they could increase the magnetic field by running electric current through a coiled wire. When they added a piece of iron through the center of the coiled wire, the magnetic field got even stronger. The electric current temporarily magnetized the piece or iron, creating an electromagnet. When the electric current stopped, the electromagnet lost its magnetism!

It is not difficult to create simple electromagnet, or temporary magnet. First, a metal wire is wrapped around an iron nail. To make a complete circuit, a wire is attached to the positive and negative ends of a battery. Rubber gloves are good to wear for insulation. As long as a current is flowing through the wire, the iron nail will remain magnetized. Once the current is turned off, it demagnetizes.

1. Use the text to determine whether each statement is **true (T)** or **false (F)**. Rewrite each false statement to be true.
   A. _____ An electric current has its own form of magnetism.
   B. _____ Magnets can be used to create electricity.
   C. _____ the magnetic field of an electric current decreases when wrapped around an iron core.
2. Describe the series of discoveries that led to a the invention of an electromagnet
3. A Use the text to define magnetize and demagnetize.
   B. Are these two words best described as synonyms or antonyms?
4. Use information from the 3rd paragraph to draw a diagram of a simple electromagnet. Label each part and explain its function.

Electricity Vocabulary

Scavenger Hunt: Use your sleuthing skills to find the meaning of the following words in this book.

Vocabulary Word	Definition
electricity	
electron	
static electricity	
conductor	
insulator	
battery	
circuit	
voltage	
amps	
series vs. parallel circuit	
open vs. closed circuit	
generator	
magnetism	

Correlations to Common Core State Standards

For your convenience, correlations are listed page-by-page, and for the entire book!

This book is correlated to the Common Core State Standards for English Language Arts grades 3-8, and to Common Core State Standards for Literacy in History, Science, & Technological Subjects grades 6-8.

Correlations are highlighted in gray.

PAGE #	READING *Includes:* RI: Reading Informational Text RST: Reading Science & Technical Subjects	WRITING *Includes:* W: Writing WHST: Writing History/Social Studies, Science, & Technical Subjects	LANGUAGE *Includes:* L: Language LF: Language Foundational Skills	SPEAKING & LISTENING *Includes:* SL: Speaking & Listening
2	RI RST · 1 2 3 4 5 6 7 8 9 10	W WHST · 1 2 3 4 5 6 7 8 9 10	L LF · 1 2 3 4 5 6	SL . 1 2 3 4 5 6
3	RI RST · 1 2 3 4 5 6 7 8 9 10	W WHST · 1 2 3 4 5 6 7 8 9 10	L LF · 1 2 3 4 5 6	SL . 1 2 3 4 5 6
4	RI RST · 1 2 3 4 5 6 7 8 9 10	W WHST · 1 2 3 4 5 6 7 8 9 10	L LF · 1 2 3 4 5 6	SL . 1 2 3 4 5 6
5	RI RST · 1 2 3 4 5 6 7 8 9 10	W WHST · 1 2 3 4 5 6 7 8 9 10	L LF · 1 2 3 4 5 6	SL . 1 2 3 4 5 6
6-7	RI RST · 1 2 3 4 5 6 7 8 9 10	W WHST · 1 2 3 4 5 6 7 8 9 10	L LF · 1 2 3 4 5 6	SL . 1 2 3 4 5 6
8	RI RST · 1 2 3 4 5 6 7 8 9 10	W WHST · 1 2 3 4 5 6 7 8 9 10	L LF · 1 2 3 4 5 6	SL . 1 2 3 4 5 6
9	RI RST · 1 2 3 4 5 6 7 8 9 10	W WHST · 1 2 3 4 5 6 7 8 9 10	L LF · 1 2 3 4 5 6	SL . 1 2 3 4 5 6
10	RI RST · 1 2 3 4 5 6 7 8 9 10	W WHST · 1 2 3 4 5 6 7 8 9 10	L LF · 1 2 3 4 5 6	SL . 1 2 3 4 5 6
11	RI RST · 1 2 3 4 5 6 7 8 9 10	W WHST · 1 2 3 4 5 6 7 8 9 10	L LF · 1 2 3 4 5 6	SL . 1 2 3 4 5 6
12-13	RI RST · 1 2 3 4 5 6 7 8 9 10	W WHST · 1 2 3 4 5 6 7 8 9 10	L LF · 1 2 3 4 5 6	SL . 1 2 3 4 5 6
14	RI RST · 1 2 3 4 5 6 7 8 9 10	W WHST · 1 2 3 4 5 6 7 8 9 10	L LF · 1 2 3 4 5 6	SL . 1 2 3 4 5 6
15	RI RST · 1 2 3 4 5 6 7 8 9 10	W WHST · 1 2 3 4 5 6 7 8 9 10	L LF · 1 2 3 4 5 6	SL . 1 2 3 4 5 6
16-17	RI RST · 1 2 3 4 5 6 7 8 9 10	W WHST · 1 2 3 4 5 6 7 8 9 10	L LF · 1 2 3 4 5 6	SL . 1 2 3 4 5 6
18-19	RI RST · 1 2 3 4 5 6 7 8 9 10	W WHST · 1 2 3 4 5 6 7 8 9 10	L LF · 1 2 3 4 5 6	SL . 1 2 3 4 5 6
20-21	RI RST · 1 2 3 4 5 6 7 8 9 10	W WHST · 1 2 3 4 5 6 7 8 9 10	L LF · 1 2 3 4 5 6	SL . 1 2 3 4 5 6
22	RI RST · 1 2 3 4 5 6 7 8 9 10	W WHST · 1 2 3 4 5 6 7 8 9 10	L LF · 1 2 3 4 5 6	SL . 1 2 3 4 5 6
23	RI RST · 1 2 3 4 5 6 7 8 9	W WHST · 1 2 3 4 5 6 7 8 9 10	L LF · 1 2 3 4 5 6	SL . 1 2 3 4 5 6
23	RI RST · 1 2 3 4 5 6 7 8 9 10	W WHST · 1 2 3 4 5 6 7 8 9 10	L LF · 1 2 3 4 5 6	SL . 1 2 3 4 5 6
COMPLETE BOOK	RI RST · 1 2 3 4 5 6 7 8 9 10	W WHST · 1 2 3 4 5 6 7 8 9 10	L LF · 1 2 3 4 5 6	SL . 1 2 3 4 5 6

For the complete Common Core standard identifier, combine your grade + "." + letter code above + "." + number code above.

In addition to the correlations indicated here, the activities may be adapted or expanded to align to additional standards and to meet the diverse needs of your unique students!